Money Makes You Happy

A play

Francis Beckett

Samuel French — London
www.samuelfrench-london.co.uk

© 2008 BY FRANCIS BECKETT

Rights of Performance by Amateurs are controlled by Samuel French Ltd, 52 Fitzroy Street, London W1T 5JR, and they, or their authorized agents, issue licences to amateurs on payment of a fee. **It is an infringement of the Copyright to give any performance or public reading of the play before the fee has been paid and the licence issued.**

The Royalty Fee indicated below is subject to contract and subject to variation at the sole discretion of Samuel French Ltd.

        Basic fee for each and every
        performance by amateurs   Code D
        in the British Isles

> **The publication of this play does not imply that it is necessarily available for performance by amateurs or professionals, either in the British Isles or Overseas. Amateurs and professionals considering a production are strongly advised in their own interests to apply to the appropriate agents for written consent before starting rehearsals or booking a theatre or hall.**

ISBN 978 0 573 02388 0

The right of Francis Beckett to be identified as author of this work has been asserted by him in accordance with Section 77 of the Copyright, Designs and Patents Act 1988

Please see page iv for further copyright information

MONEY MAKES YOU HAPPY

First performed at the Bridewell Theatre, London, from 17th to 27th July 2007, and the White Bear Theatre, London, from 31st July to 5th August 2007, by Baseless Fabric Theatre Company.

Jeremy Bunter	Jamie Griffiths-Jones
Miriam	Katy Balfour
Ruth	Nicki Walsh
Hugh Houndsby	David Zezulka
Carol	Sarah J. Malter
Gary	David Zezulka
Magdela	Sarah J. Malter

Directed by Joanna Turner
Lighting and Sound Engineer Kelli Marston
Stage Manager Alex Carruth

COPYRIGHT INFORMATION
(See also page ii)

This play is fully protected under the Copyright Laws of the British Commonwealth of Nations, the United States of America and all countries of the Berne and Universal Copyright Conventions.

All rights, including Stage, Motion Picture, Radio, Television, Public Reading, and Translation into Foreign Languages, are strictly reserved.

No part of this publication may lawfully be reproduced in ANY form or by any means — photocopying, typescript, recording (including video-recording), manuscript, electronic, mechanical, or otherwise — or be transmitted or stored in a retrieval system, without prior permission.

Licences are issued subject to the understanding that it shall be made clear in all advertising matter that the audience will witness an amateur performance; that the names of the authors of the plays shall be included on all announcements and on all programmes; and that the integrity of the authors' work will be preserved.

The Royalty Fee is subject to contract and subject to variation at the sole discretion of Samuel French Ltd.

In Theatres or Halls seating Four Hundred or more the fee will be subject to negotiation.

In Territories Overseas the fee quoted in this Acting Edition may not apply. A fee will be quoted on application to our local authorized agent, or if there is no such agent, on application to Samuel French Ltd, London.

VIDEO-RECORDING OF AMATEUR PRODUCTIONS

Please note that the copyright laws governing video-recording are extremely complex and that it should not be assumed that any play may be video-recorded for *whatever purpose* without first obtaining the permission of the appropriate agents. The fact that a play is published by Samuel French Ltd does not indicate that video rights are available or that Samuel French Ltd controls such rights.

CHARACTERS

Ruth, a lawyer, about 30
Jeremy Bunter, a writer, about 30
Miriam, Ruth's sister, late 20s
Hugh Houndsby, marketing executive, 30s
Carol, contract publishing company executive, 30s
Gary Graft, political advisor, 30s
Magdela, entrepreneur, 30s

SYNOPSIS OF SCENES

The action of the play takes place in the living-room of Ruth's expensive London house

SCENE 1 One summer afternoon
SCENE 2 Late the same evening
SCENE 3 The next morning, breakfast
SCENE 4 The following evening
SCENE 5 The next morning, early
SCENE 6 11a.m. that same morning
SCENE 7 The following morning
SCENE 8 Early the same evening
SCENE 9 The following evening

Time—the present

MONEY MAKES YOU HAPPY

Scene 1

The living-room of Ruth's house in Golders Green, north London

There are two chairs and a coffee table

Jeremy enters, wearing a coat and carrying a small rucksack. He is ill at ease. Looking about him, he starts to sit on a chair

Miriam enters. She is brisk, talkative and moves all the time. She points to the other chair

Miriam That's the best chair for you.
Jeremy Oh. Oh, right-oh, then.

Jeremy moves towards the other chair and moves it, but does not sit on it

Miriam Only she likes that one herself. You know how it is, hard day, likes her own chair at the end of it. I don't know how long she'll be, could be forever if she's got a case conference. Probably shouldn't have let you in. She always says don't let strangers in. Still, too late now. Not being funny, you know, only ...
Jeremy I'm not exactly a stranger.
Miriam No, of course, I know, you said, you're ... who are you again?
Jeremy Jeremy Bunter.
Miriam Yes, that's it, you said, and you're ... Jeremy Bunter? You're not the author of *Trekking to Paradise*, are you?
Jeremy Well, yes. What a pleasure to meet someone who remembers it. It's years ago, everyone seems to have forgotten, and then —

especially someone as young as, well, as you obviously are. I could sign your copy for you, if you wanted.

Miriam I never heard of it, only Ruth showed it to me, your name on the cover, you signed her copy. Bit friendly, what you wrote. You must know her pretty well. Are you one of her lovers? I lose track, there's been so many. Sorry, didn't mean that exactly. Only it's true. Well, sort of true.

Jeremy Well ...

Miriam Anyway, I'd make you a cup of tea, only I've got to go and feed the baby.

Jeremy You have a baby?

Miriam No, her baby, silly.

Jeremy (*deeply shocked*) Ruth's baby?

Miriam She's not the only one, you know, lots of people have babies.

Jeremy But Ruth ... I'm sorry, I wasn't expecting that. She never told me. How long has this been going on — I mean, how old is the baby?

Miriam Well, I say baby — you know, they grow so fast, one minute they're lying there in their own ——

Jeremy How old is the baby?

Miriam The next day they're into everything, little terrors. Can't turn your back on them for a moment.

Jeremy How old is the baby?

Miriam Three.

Jeremy Three! She's had this baby for three years!

Miriam Well, three next birthday. Two, really.

Jeremy So you're ... you're a kind of nanny.

Miriam No way. You wouldn't want strangers looking after your baby. That's a job for family. I'm her sister.

Jeremy You're Miriam!

Miriam Told you about me, did she? That's nice. I'm living with Ruth right now, only it's just temporary, 'til I get sorted out, and I look after Ben. It suits me, and it suits her. I mean, she's all high-powered and clever and a lawyer and all that. I'm the stupid sister.

Jeremy Surely not.

Scene 1

Miriam So that's it. I'll go and feed Ben, you sit and make yourself comfortable. Read a newspaper if you like. Or a book.
Jeremy There isn't a newspaper. Or a book.
Miriam No, she hates things lying about, making the place look untidy. I meant, if you'd brought a newspaper with you. Or a book. Then you could read it.

Miriam starts to exit, then turns

Well, sit down, then. Make yourself comfortable.

Jeremy sits down. He looks as uncomfortable as it's possible to be

That's it. You don't look so untidy now.

Miriam exits

Jeremy jumps up

Jeremy Miriam! Miriam, when's Ben going to be three?
Miriam (*off*) February.

Jeremy feverishly unwraps his rucksack, gets out a notebook and pen and a small pocket diary, and begins to do calculations

Ruth enters

Jeremy does not see her

Ruth What are you doing in London? You hate the place.
Jeremy (*reacting to her*) I wanted to see you.
Ruth You could have rung.
Jeremy It was kind of a spur of the moment thing.
Ruth Yes, you're kind of a spur of the moment person. I remember that. (*Referring to the rucksack*) What's that doing there?

Jeremy launches into what is clearly a prepared speech. As he speaks, he turns to face the audience and does not see Ruth

During the following, Ruth picks up his rucksack, examines it with distaste and exits

Jeremy I've always wondered what your home looked like. Odd, we shared so much and I never saw the place you lived in. You appeared like magic at Solva station on Friday nights, always so pleased to see me, a gift from heaven. I'd take you sailing, we'd have a few pints in the Royal George and go home to bed. Then you came less and less, and then you stopped coming at all. And I thought it didn't bother me, I pottered round the village, wrote a chapter or two, didn't like it, tore it up. But I found myself wondering, and I woke up this morning and I thought: I'd really like to know why she's not coming to Solva any more. (*As he reaches this triumphant finale, he turns round, just in time to see Ruth*)

Ruth enters, carrying two cups of tea and hands one of them to Jeremy

Ruth I suppose you want to know why I stopped coming to Solva.
Jeremy It did cross my mind, yes.
Ruth Not easy with a small baby.
Jeremy I bought you something.

Jeremy reaches for his rucksack, which no longer there

Where's my ——
Ruth In the cupboard. Can't have it on the floor, making the place look like a campsite.

Jeremy goes to put his tea on the table

Use a coaster, you'll stain the table.

Ruth moves a coaster towards him and he puts his tea on it

Jeremy Yes, well, I didn't know about the baby, did I? I mean, it's not something I'd forget. I don't think. You didn't tell me, did you?

Scene 1

Jeremy waits. Ruth occupies herself about the room, plumping cushions, picking up Jeremy's papers and putting them in a neat heap, and does not seem inclined to answer

    I didn't think you were keen on having children.
Ruth I wasn't. I didn't intend to, but you have to deal with realities.
Jeremy You could have ...
Ruth Yes, I could have. But it wasn't a bad moment, professionally, to take a few months out. So I decided to have the baby.
Jeremy Do you remember that summer, that last summer we spent together?
Ruth Yes, I think about that summer, sometimes.
Jeremy We were happy then. I think.
Ruth Yes.
Jeremy And fairly soon after that ...
Ruth I stopped coming. It was time.
Jeremy Time for what?
Ruth Just time. Where are you staying in London?
Jeremy Ah. Well. Well, I could go and stay with — I've got a friend in Shepherd's Bush. I suppose I could see if he'll put me up.
Ruth Are you staying long?
Jeremy No. Tonight, maybe tomorrow night.
Ruth That's OK then, you can stay here. There's a spare room. So long as it's just for a night or two.

Ruth picks up the teacups and goes out. Jeremy fails to see she's gone

Jeremy Really? Oh, good, I wasn't — you don't have to, I can always get myself sorted out. Only I admit I've got a marked preference ...

He notices she's gone

    I always hated it when she did that.

Black-out

Scene 2

The same

Ruth is dressed more casually and Jeremy has discarded his coat. They are sitting at the coffee table with a bottle of wine between them

Ruth Yes, of course Ben could be your child. What difference would it make?

Jeremy Is he like me?

Ruth In some ways, but I think I can train him out of that. Look, Jeremy, having a small child doesn't exactly fit your lifestyle, does it? So long as you've got the price of a pint, and a rented room to rest your head, you're happy. I mean, Jeremy, I'm terribly fond of you, but working doesn't figure a lot in your life, does it?

Jeremy Well, I have been working on the sequel to *Trekking to Paradise*.

Ruth You've been working on it for ten years. Ever since *Trekking to Paradise* came out, and you were the handsome young toast of literary London. And how much have you written?

Jeremy Well, I've thrown most of it away.

Ruth How much?

Jeremy I've written the first chapter. Well, part of it, anyway.

Ruth In the morning you put in a full stop, and in the afternoon you take it out again.

Jeremy Well, full stops matter.

Ruth I gave you the name of an agent I knew. Did you talk to her?

Jeremy Yes. Not to any good effect, I'm afraid.

Ruth What did she say?

Jeremy She said, "Look, Jeremy, your strength is young people. Backpackers in search of Utopia. Get back to that. And this time, can you make the young people Americans?'

Ruth Maybe she was right.

Jeremy Ruth. I was a student when I wrote *Trekking to Paradise*. I write about different things now.

Ruth You're still trying to make the money you made from *Trekking*

Scene 2

to Paradise last a few more months. Church mice give you handouts from the collection.

Jeremy I work.

Ruth Sometimes you write an article, and from time to time you sell one. You're not exactly prime father material.

Jeremy Do all fathers have to be accountants or lawyers?

Ruth No, but it helps. Look, Jeremy, I think the world of you, but this child arrived and I thought, I either do this on my own, or I do it with a man who's grounded, who's serious about life, who's going to make some money and be some sort of rock for me. Not a kind of cheerful butterfly, sitting in a village on a lovely stretch of the Pembrokeshire coast and thinking, "Tomorrow I'll write the definitive twenty-first century novel", pint in one hand and spliff in the other.

Jeremy I suppose proper fathers have a latte in one hand and a mobile phone in the other. You must have seen something in me you liked.

Ruth I thought you were exotic. Public school, English, languid — what did you care about security? We didn't meet people like you in Stoke Newington.

Jeremy I though you were exotic. East End girl made good, Jewish, driven, organized — what did you care about creativity? We didn't meet people like you in Herefordshire.

Ruth You were hunting and holy communion.

Jeremy You were persecution and *pesach*.

Ruth It was time to move on.

Jeremy Were you going to tell me about the baby?

Ruth No.

Jeremy Were you ever going to see me again?

Ruth I suppose I assumed you'd find a replacement quite fast. You were great for romantic weekends — even a whole summer — in a pretty seaside fishing village. But with a child, I wanted a *mensch* or no one.

Jeremy Maybe you could turn me into a *mensch*.

Ruth Too big a job.

Jeremy Did you find a replacement for me?

Ruth It wasn't like that exactly, was it? I mean, we had a strictly weekend romance. What we did in the week …

Jeremy I didn't do anything much in the week.

Ruth rises and picks up the wine bottle and the glasses

There's still some in the bottle.

He stands and takes a glass from her, then moves behind her and puts one arm round her waist, holding the other hand with the glass in it in front of her. She fills it, then tries to remove his arm. He resists. He takes the wine bottle from her and pours the rest into his glass

Ruth A *mensch* wouldn't drain the bottle.

Jeremy gives her the glass, untouched

Ruth takes wine and glasses and exits

Black-out

Scene 3

The same. The next morning, at breakfast

Miriam enters carrying a tray with three mugs. She puts the tray down on the table

Miriam (*calling*) Coffee! Shall I give Ben his breakfast? It's nearly time for you to go.

Ruth enters

Where's Ben? You haven't left him with ...
Ruth Couldn't tear them apart. Jeremy's explaining existentialism and Ben's blowing bubbles. Or maybe it was the other way round.
Miriam You've left Jeremy looking after Ben? But he ... he's not ... he wouldn't know what to do if — Jeremy's not Jewish, is he?
Ruth Miriam, non-Jewish people have been bringing up children for quite a few years now. He'll be fine.
Miriam Well, if you're sure. He's a bit vague, isn't he, and I mean, well, he's a man. He wouldn't know what to do if ... and Ben's only

Scene 3

really used to you and me. He might find it a bit strange being left with this strange man.
Ruth Oh, all right, you can rescue Ben.
Miriam Jeremy won't feed him. They don't grow if you don't feed them.

She goes out, and comes straight back in, shocked

Jeremy's put this huge mound of food in front of him. Forcing all that down him! Poor little thing, he's only got a little stomach.

Jeremy enters

Jeremy Perhaps I should leave things to Miriam.
Miriam He's not a horse, you know.

Miriam exits

Ruth She likes to organize things in her own way.
Jeremy Do you think young Ben liked me?
Ruth Seemed to. You were a bit different from what he's used to, anyway.
Jeremy He's a bit young to notice that.
Ruth I mean, he doesn't see many men. Certainly not ones who want to talk to him about existentialism.
Jeremy He seemed interested. Perhaps I confused him with the difference between Sartre and Camus.
Ruth Perhaps.
Jeremy Ruth, listen to me. I want to stay with you. I can still write like a dream. I can write whatever the world will pay for. Marketing jargon, tabloid journalism, any old crap. I don't because it doesn't suit me, but I'd do it for you.

Ruth picks up the tray of coffee mugs and goes out

(*Calling*) I used to think it was prostituting myself, doing that, but we're all prostitutes. Are you listening?

Ruth returns

Ruth You used to say it was prostituting yourself, doing that.
Jeremy I hate it when you do that.
Ruth I know.
Jeremy Can I stay tonight?
Ruth Any particular reason?
Jeremy There's something I was thinking of going to in London tomorrow.
Ruth What?
Jeremy You'll laugh. It's the old public school. The old boys' dinner.
Ruth But you hated the place. You said it was all ——
Jeremy Beating, bullying, bigotry and buggery. But they stick together. An old boy wants a job, there's some rich chaps there who'll give him one. There's a chap called Hugh Houndsby.
Ruth A friend of yours?
Jeremy No, I hate the sight of him. Thick, rich rugger player. Used to knock me about every time he found me writing poetry. But he runs a marketing company and he needs writers. He's going to be at the dinner, and I'll talk to him afterwards. Can I stay?
Ruth Yes, you can stay. But just one more night, I don't want you getting comfortable here.

Black-out

Scene 4

The same. The following evening

Hugh Houndsby stumbles in, fairly drunk but not incapable. Jeremy follows

Hugh They do us well, the East India Club. So where's that Armagnac I was promised?
Jeremy Ah. Yes. Must have put it somewhere.

Jeremy goes out. During the following he returns with bottle of Armagnac and two glasses

Scene 4

Hugh (*shouting after him*) You haven't done so badly for yourself after all. Nice house in Golders Green, you'd get three quarters of a million k for this, no trouble. Bought it at the bottom of the market, I hope.
Jeremy Ah. This. Yes. Well, actually ——
Hugh You going to pour that stuff, or just wave it about? Here, give it to me.

Jeremy hands the bottle to Hugh, who looks at it and then pours

Hugh Not bad. Not the best, but a cool fifty pounds a bottle. Who'd have thought it — Jeremy Bunter's made a bob or two. Famous author. What's that bloody book called again?
Jeremy *Trekking to Paradise.*
Hugh *Trekking to Paradise.* Well, anyway. Means you can string a few words together. You always could, of course. Used to write poetry at school, didn't you?
Jeremy No. I mean, yes, sometimes.
Hugh Doesn't shift a lot of widgets, poetry.
Jeremy Shift a lot of widgets?
Hugh Not a good marketing tool. Still, you can scribble. One word after another. And what do you want from your old mate Hugh?
Jeremy Well, this is the thing, Hugh. I've reached a crossroads. It's ten years since *Trekking for Paradise.* The next novel just isn't coming. I don't know why. There's a kind of lacuna.
Hugh Went to Laguna last year. Lot to be said for the Maldives. Overrated, of course.
Jeremy Yes. I think it's more that I need a stint in the real world, a time to recharge my creativity. And that's why I thought of you. I thought: Hugh wants people who can write good utilitarian copy. And then, of course, there's the money. I mean, the revenue stream from *Trekking to Paradise* has started to dry up.
Hugh Didn't do you badly. All this. (*Gesturing vaguely about the room*) All yours. Not bad.
Jeremy Well. Yes, it did me well. But I don't feel I'm ready for that sort of work again. So I thought ...
Hugh You thought you'd talk to me. Quite right too. I'm not going to send an old college chap away empty-handed, that's not my way,

even if — we weren't exactly close, were we? But who the hell cares. You're college.

Hugh lurches towards Jeremy, appearing to be about to punch him. Jeremy instinctively cowers and covers his face

Jeremy Sorry. Yes, that's — that's good of you.
Hugh No problem. If I can't help an old college chap in trouble, what's it all for? I've built up this company from scratch, Jeremy. I've built it up by sheer work and determination and know-how.
Jeremy Oh, I see. I always thought it was your father's company.
Hugh Well, he started the thing, of course he did, but he didn't make it what it is today. I started right from the bottom.
Jeremy I heard he left you six million pounds.
Hugh Well, not six million smackers in my hand. It was all wrapped up in the business, old son. I had to get down there, get my hands dirty, take some risks. I'm a risk-taker, Jeremy. Business is worth a hell of a lot more than six million now, I'll tell you that for nothing.
Jeremy Is it? Oh, well done, Hugh.
Hugh Six and a half million, I kid you not. See, my father, he was an entrepreneur of the old-fashioned type. No MBAs in his day. No real focus on shareholder value. Not good enough. These days, to be a successful entrepreneur, you need the right letters after your name. Everyone knows a guy with an MBA knows what he's talking about. So when I took over the business, I knew what to do. Lot of dead wood in the company in those days. No dead wood in my company now. Know what business is like today, Jeremy?
Jeremy Don't think I do, Hugh. Tell me.
Hugh It's like climbing the north face of the Eiger — You could slip off any moment. It's like being on the front line in Afghanistan — The enemy's out there somewhere. It keeps me pretty busy, just zapping the opposition. I need to hire chaps to do the simple things. You're a scribbler. I need scribblers. Haven't the time to do it myself.
Jeremy No, of course. You must be a very busy man.
Hugh There's writers, Jeremy, and then there's doers. I'm a doer. If I want a writer, I go into the corridor — figuratively speaking you understand — I go into the corridor outside my office and I shout

Scene 4

"Hack!" and some little chap comes running, licking his pencil, touching his forelock. Can you spell "innovative"?

Jeremy Can I spell it? Well, yes, I think I can.

Hugh And "superb"? And "excellence"?

Jeremy I'm quite good at spelling, Hugh, if you remember.

Hugh Proper writers, we need. Tight marketing copy, not a word that doesn't earn its living. Can you do that?

Jeremy I can do that.

Hugh Right. Here's the deal. You work from home. It's good for you, you don't have to leave your three quarters of a million quid house, and it's good for me because I don't have to pay for your computer and pay bloody London rates for office space for you. You'll be on a freelance contract so I can fire you whenever I like, and you get paid what I feel like paying you. Right?

Jeremy Sounds perfect.

Hugh No need to thank me, it's the least I can do. College man. Fine old place, the college.

Jeremy Well, it had its dark side, Hugh. You must admit.

Hugh What the hell do you mean?

Jeremy Well, you must remember. There was a nasty business with some of the teachers, and a pretty awkward report which they hushed up. I thought of writing an article about it sometime.

Hugh If you mean what I think you mean, Jeremy, old son, then you won't breathe a word to anyone, anywhere, ever, about that, unless you want to find yourself hanging from Nelson's Column by your bollocks.

Jeremy I thought most people knew.

Hugh If they do, they keep bloody quiet. Get the college a bad name. Only dogs shit on their own doorstep. You bloody keep that to yourself. No one bloody talks about it, right. You come to the old boys' dinners and you smile and chatter away, and you don't even let yourself know you know about that. Otherwise we'll all piss on you, unless you happen to be on fire, in which case we'll keep our piss to ourselves. Am I making myself clear?

Jeremy Painfully so, Hugh. Painfully so.

Hugh Good. Was that your first old boys' dinner tonight? I go every year. Best bit, when we stand up over the brandy and sing the college

song. Let's do the chorus one last time, then you can call me a taxi.
Jeremy What, now?
Hugh All right, quietly, don't want to wake the little lady upstairs. There is one, isn't there?
Jeremy Well, yes, and she's ——
Hugh (*singing at the top of his voice*)
> United as our faith contrives,
> Our debt we now acknowledge,
> To those three pillars of our lives,
> God, family and college.

Ruth appears in her dressing gown, looking thunderous

Black-out

Scene 5

The same. The next morning

Miriam and Ruth are on stage. Ruth is dressed for work, holding a coffee

Ruth They collect the rubbish this morning. You need to get it all outside and pay the milkman, there's money in the desk drawer. Give Ben the puréed fish I made for lunch, it's good for his brains. You can let Jeremy sleep 'til nine-thirty but no later. He's got someone coming to see him at eleven.
Miriam He was drunk last night, wasn't he?
Ruth Not as drunk as the oaf he brought home with him.
Miriam But he offered Jeremy a job. I heard him. Well, I couldn't sleep, the racket they were making. That's good, isn't it? I mean, any kind of job would be good, wouldn't it? He's got to work, I mean, it stands to reason, not trying to be funny about your boyfriend. I mean ——
Ruth He's not my boyfriend. And I'm not having him work for that oaf.
Miriam Only don't you think …

Ruth exits, carrying the coffee cup

Scene 6

No, obviously you don't.

Ruth comes back

I mean, it's better than nothing. Though I hope you're not thinking of ... I mean, it's none of my business of course, but you know, if you're thinking that Ben ought to have a man about the house, well, I mean, it wouldn't be Jeremy. I don't mean I don't like him, of course, but he isn't exactly ...

Ruth I wasn't.

Miriam No, I know, but I mean if you were, well, you'd want one who was more of a sort of role model than Jeremy, wouldn't you? I mean, being really honest, Ruth, could you say he was a *mensch*? I mean, I know Dad always says you're not playing fair by Ben, not having a father figure, but he wasn't thinking of someone like Jeremy, he was thinking of a nice Jewish accountant.

Ruth You talk such rubbish all the time. (*Putting her coat on; making to leave*) Tell Jeremy I've made an appointment for him to see Carol.

Miriam You're not feeding him to Carol. She'll eat him alive.

Ruth She's coming at eleven. She'll be on time. Make sure he's presentable.

Ruth exits

Black-out

Scene 6

The same

Miriam enters with Carol, who is carrying a bag

Miriam He'll be down, Carol, he's just making himself presentable. You know what they're like, some of them anyway. He had a heavy night.

Carol Did he now?

Miriam Oh dear, I probably wasn't supposed to tell you that. You know what I'm like.

Carol Don't worry about it for an instant, darling. You know how much we all love you for it. I think he's here.

Jeremy enters. He's made an effort, put on a shirt and tie, but he looks rough. Miriam goes to him and straightens his tie

Miriam I said to call me to come and have a look at you before you came out.
Carol He's fine, Miriam, just fine. Geniuses are supposed to be a little dishevelled. What a privilege to meet the great author! It's one of my favourite books, *Walking to Heaven*.
Jeremy *Trekking to Paradise*.
Carol So wonderful to meet you in the flesh. Such a thrill. You've been one of my idols over the years.
Jeremy Well, that's wonderful. Would you like me to sign your copy of the book?
Carol I haven't got it with me, darling.
Jeremy No, but I'll happily meet you one day and sign it. I don't often get to meet real fans, not these days.
Carol As a matter of fact, Jeremy darling, I remember now, I lent it to someone. I loved it so much, I said to my friend, darling you simply must read this simply marvellous travelogue.
Jeremy Novel.
Carol And she must have loved it so much she couldn't bear to give it back to me. It's OK, Miriam, you can leave him with me, I won't eat him.

As Miriam passes Jeremy she cups her hand over her mouth and whispers to him

Miriam I don't think she's read it at all.
Jeremy Really?

Miriam exits

Carol Now, Jeremy, I don't know how much Ruth told you.
Jeremy Not a thing. She was in a hurry.

Scene 6

Carol Yes, she's always in a hurry, our Ruth. Of course we all love her to bits, don't we, but perhaps a shade brusque. Now, I run a contract publishing company. Big organizations come to us with their publishing needs, and we fulfil them. Magazines, reports, electronic publishing, whatever they need. So of course we need writers. And when Ruth said that the great Jeremy Bunter might be available for a little freelancing, well, naturally I jumped at the chance.

Jeremy Naturally.

Carol Of course, our clients will tell you what to write.

Jeremy Of course.

Carol And how to write it.

Jeremy I see.

Carol And which words to use.

Jeremy Which words?

Carol But you write it. Using your unique brilliance at writing. It's your creativity we want. But also using the words they like. They like words like "innovative".

Jeremy So I've heard.

Carol And "excellence". And "superb". So you use them a lot. Can you do that?

Jeremy I can do that, Carol. I can have excellence coming out of every pore.

Carol Marvellous!

Jeremy Only, well, I'd really want to do it properly, so, well — what am I contributing? I mean, if they supply the words, what do I supply?

Carol Good thinking, Jeremy darling. What's your added value? We're going to get on. You're on my wavelength. The answer's simple, darling, you supply your unique brilliance, and we present it to them in a nice PowerPoint presentation with graphics that jump up and down to hold their attention, and we serve coffee out of nice cups, and petits fours, while they listen to you telling them whatever they want to hear. So, you see, you're adding value. Lots and lots of value.

Jeremy Yes. Well, that's clear enough.

Carol What is it, darling? I want you to be totally, totally happy with this.

Jeremy Well, tell me if I'm being stupid, but if they're supplying the words, they might as well write it themselves, surely.

Carol Jeremy, these are top people. They don't have time to sit down and write things. That's what they pay you for. Look, Jeremy, darling, I know it's a challenge for a creative genius to adapt to the disciplines of client publishing.

Jeremy It's not a challenge, it's just a difficulty.

Carol Challenge, darling. We don't say "difficulty", we say "challenge". You'll soon get the hang of the vocabulary. Even if it's sometimes challenging.

Jeremy Yes, well, I'm sure that won't be a problem.

Carol There are no problems, darling, only solutions. Sometimes the solutions come first, too. We often have a solution before we've identified a challenge, then the challenge is to find the challenge to which our solution is the solution. Are you with me?

Jeremy I think so.

Carol We need solutions people. Are you a solutions person, Jeremy?

Jeremy Well, yes, of course, I'm all in favour of solutions. Only, well, I do like words to mean what they say.

Carol Oh, do you?

Jeremy You know what happens to words when you misuse them? I went to the local swimming pool yesterday. They used to have a changing room. You know what they call it now? They call it the "changing village". They think they're turning a hot, sweaty, smelly place with ugly iron lockers into a rural idyll. But they're not. They're making "village" mean a hot, sweaty, smelly place with ugly iron lockers. They're vandalizing the language.

Carol Look, darling, it's lovely to meet you. A very special privilege for me, I'm such an admirer of your work. But this isn't going to work, is it? It would be a desecration of your wonderful genius to have you working for me, wouldn't it?

Jeremy No. No, really, I think I can deal with the prob — I mean, I'm up to the challenge. Yes, you know, I really think I am. Do we like "mouth-watering"?

Carol Only for food products, darling. With them we can really let rip. Bread is always crusty, meat always juicy, wine always full-bodied. Like women. Oh, darling, you have to inhabit our world. You have to really, really inhabit it. Can you do that, darling?

Scene 6

Jeremy I think so.

Carol I hope so. Because I'm going to give this a chance. You're seeing your first client tomorrow.

Jeremy Tomorrow?

Carol I believe in throwing people in the deep end, darling. I'm going to tell Magdela you're her new writer. She's the right client for you. And she'll be so pleased when I tell her she's getting a famous writer. Darling, you'll just love Magdela.

Jeremy Who is she?

Carol Magdela, darling, is the utterly brilliant entrepreneur who founded *Stagestruck: The Academy for Talented Toddlers*. You'll see her franchises everywhere. Well, not everywhere. They're not cheap, you don't get them in the slums and the immigrant areas, but everywhere you'd ever want to go. They send their little darlings to Magdela's classes every Saturday morning, where they learn to act and sing and dance, so they all grow up to be famous film stars just like they always dreamed they would.

Jeremy What can I do for her?

Carol I said to Magdela, what you need is a magazine to send out to all the little dears. She said, "But they're already paying us, why bother with them? I should be reaching the people who aren't paying me yet." So I said, of course, you're right, Magdela, how I wish I had your sharp clarity of vision. Such an education just talking to you. On the other hand, there's below-the-line PR and synergy and ——

Jeremy Not sure I know what that means.

Carol No need to worry about that, darling. Public relations language is a bit challenging sometimes. I think Magdela had trouble with the words but she didn't ask, she just said "fine". So we're going to. And you, darling, are going to be her first editor. Just so long as she takes to you. She's bound to, darling. I expect you have women falling at your feet all the time. Here's a tip, darling. Don't contradict her, whatever she says.

Jeremy Don't contradict her? What, never?

Carol Never. Never, never, never. Whatever she says. She's a very successful businesswoman, she's bound to be always right. Now, I've got all the material she wants you to read. (*Taking papers from her bag and handing them to Jeremy*) And by the time you see her I want you to have some drafts ready for her, so she can see that you really are the genius I'm going to tell her you are. And that's about it, darling. Must rush, I've got a client lunch. Bye. (*She kisses him on both cheeks; calling out as she leaves*) Bye, Miriam.

Carol exits and we hear the front door shut

Jeremy stands, uncertain, leafing through the papers

The doorbell rings

Gary (*off*) Miriam. Great to see you again.

Gary and Miriam enter. Gary is carrying a huge bundle of papers

Miriam Jeremy, this is Gary, he's awfully important in the government or something like that. Only Ruth's not here. We'll have to entertain him 'til she gets back.
Jeremy So long as he promises not to call me darling.
Gary You have my solemn word on it. Gary Graft. It was you I wanted to see anyway.

He holds his hand out. Jeremy takes it absent-mindedly and Gary shakes hands vigorously

Jeremy Me? Well, it's nice to see you, Mr Graft. I expect.
Gary Good to meet you, Jerry.
Jeremy Jeremy.
Gary Look, I need to come to the point, Jerry. I've only been able to allocate half an hour to this meeting.
Jeremy This is a meeting?
Gary Miriam, don't you have to wipe Ben's bottom or something? This is business.
Miriam Ben, no. He's resting, I can — Oh, I see, you want to talk alone. I'd better go and see if Ben's all right or something, hadn't I?

Scene 6

Gary Yes.

Miriam exits

During the following, Ruth enters and stands US, *unnoticed*

Right. I'm the Political Adviser to the Secretary of State for Schools. We want you to edit a magazine for teachers. Here's the contract. Got it double quick out of the civil service. (*Handing over the bundle of papers*) Need your signature at the bottom and the first cheque will be in the post within the month.
Ruth What on earth would you do that for?
Jeremy Ruth. I wasn't expecting you yet.
Ruth Court finished early. Thought I'd come and see how it went with Carol.
Jeremy This is ——
Ruth I know Gary Graft.
Gary And of course everyone knows the delectable Ruth.
Jeremy Everyone seems to know everyone. I always thought London was a big place. It's just like Solva.
Ruth If you're a politician who sails close to the law, I'm the sort of lawyer you get to know.
Gary Ruth and I, we're old friends. Old, old friends. We've watched the sun come up over Hyde Park together, Ruth and I, haven't we?
Ruth Not often. What do you want him to do and what are you offering?
Gary The department produces a magazine for teachers.
Jeremy You want me to be the editor?
Gary Well, not exactly, that's a bit specialized, bit delicate how you phrase things. Got one of the biggest PR consultancies in London to do that. We have to tell them exactly what to write.
Jeremy So why don't you just write it yourself?
Gary Got to have the private sector in, Jerry. Government policy. But we can't let them actually do anything, because we're a bit fussy about the words we use. Politically delicate.
Jeremy So if the consultancy doesn't do much, what do you want me to do?

Gary We'd like you as a kind of consultant really.
Jeremy A consultant to the consultancy?
Gary That's the idea. Magazine comes out four times a year. You'd be a sort of editorial consultant. Cast a professional eye over the words, send us an email telling us what you think. Your general impression. You know?
Jeremy Just four times a year?
Gary That's it.
Jeremy Four times a year I'd look at a few articles and tell you what I think of them?
Gary That's the general idea, yes. Value your opinion.
Ruth How much are you offering him?
Gary Thirty thousand pounds a year on a four year contract.
Jeremy It's a deal. Where do I sign?
Ruth (*taking contract from Jeremy*) Where do I find the catch? Don't make me read the whole thing.
Gary Paragraph 57F(3).
Ruth (*finding the catch*) It's just a gagging clause. (*To Jeremy*) What do you know that Gary wants you to keep *shtum* about?

Jeremy shrugs

Gary Look, Ruth, it's like this. We've got a mutual friend, Jez and I. Hugh Houndsby. Now, it appears that Jezzo and Hughie had a bit of a heart to heart last night.
Ruth That's one way of putting it.
Gary During the course of which Jerry here made reference to a rather unpleasant scandal at his old school.
Jeremy (*to Ruth*) A few pretty nasty things happened. It was that sort of place — three hundred boys in a boarding school, pretty amateurish teachers, crumbling and Dickensian. All it ever had to offer was snob value.
Gary That's exactly the sort of little speech we don't want you making, ever, to anyone, again.
Ruth Why not? What does it matter to you? Or your political masters?

Scene 6

Gary Look, we're talking deep, deep background, you understand? This is so far off the record that it's out of sight. But I'm told a few publishers and editors still remember Jeremy Bunter, and he might be thinking of writing about those events. And if someone starts saying unhelpful things about his old school, this will be a considerable embarrassment to the Secretary of State. My job is to make sure the Secretary of State isn't embarrassed.

Ruth Why? This was a public school. Not a state school. Nothing to do with the government at all. What does the government care about its reputation?

Gary All right. I'll tell you as much as I can, and then a bit more that I shouldn't, and you'll have to imagine the rest. You must have heard of our new education policy. We call it "Excellence From Innovation."

Jeremy Is it challenging, by any chance?

Gary Well done, Jerry. That's the subtitle. "Challenges for a Young Country."

Jeremy A young country?

Gary Young is a good word. Voters like young.

Ruth What's it about?

Gary The name says it all, really. You know what Britain's state schools are like. Concrete jungles filled with drug-crazed teenagers with communists for teachers, where the kids all grow up to be terrorists. Now, private schools like yours are the exact opposite. Kids sit in neat rows, wear nice, new uniforms, do what they're told, say "Yes sir, no sir, three bags full sir" and go to Oxford. So how do we make state schools like the private schools? How do we bottle what they've got and give it to the hoi polloi?

Jeremy Simple. Give all the hoi polloi six figure incomes so they can send their children to the posh schools.

Gary Not that simple. There's another way. Ruth knows what I mean.

Ruth You give private schools lots of money in return for telling the state schools how to have all the children sitting in neat rows, wearing nice, new uniforms, doing what they're told, saying "Yes sir, no sir, three bags full sir" and going to Oxford. And of course, the only private schools which will take your money are the failing ones, like Jeremy's old school, who need the money.

Gary That's it. All clear now?

Jeremy I still don't see where I come in. Not that I mind coming in, at that sort of price.

Ruth I suspect that some time quite soon, Gary's boss will be announcing the name of the first private school to get a huge government handout so it can go and tell state schools its secret. And I rather fear that it's going to be one you know rather well.

Gary I couldn't confirm or deny that, you know. Not even off the record. But whatever school is chosen, it's going to get twenty million pounds of taxpayers' money. Wouldn't want anyone thinking we're putting it into a crumbling, scandal-ridden wreck of a place, would we?

Jeremy That's quite, quite mad. I mean, at the college they were useless. The kids in any self-respecting comprehensive would make mincemeat of my old teachers.

Gary That's another speech we'd rather you didn't make again. I think you'll find it comes under the general prohibition outlined in Paragraph 57F(3), which is fairly widely drafted. We don't want people saying my political boss has wasted twenty million pounds on some incompetent, pampered little boarding school where the head lost the plot years ago. And there are some people who would say that, make no mistake.

Jeremy I imagine there are. I could imagine myself saying it.

Gary You could have a substantially more comfortable life for the next four years if you don't. Do we have a deal? Because if we don't, it will become my painful duty to make sure everyone knows that you're a fantasist with a grudge, and no one should ever employ you to do anything ever again, or publish a single word you ever write.

Ruth Gary, you could never resist making threats. There are still a few places where they don't blacklist someone because people like you put the word out.

Gary Not as many as you'd think. So what are you going to do, Jerry?

Jeremy (*looking at Ruth*) What do you think?

Scene 7

Ruth Your choice. I just wanted to make sure you knew what you were signing.
Gary You can call me. But don't leave it too long. Can't keep an offer like this open forever. By the way, if you're interested in a peerage later on, and you keep your nose clean, well, you never know your luck. Bye now.

Gary exits

Ruth and Jeremy look at each other

Black-out

Scene 7

The same

Jeremy and Magdela are on stage. Magdela is looking through some sheets of paper

Magdela Is this the best you can do? I thought you were supposed to be a writer.
Jeremy I thought it was good.
Magdela It's crap.
Jeremy Well, I knew it was one or the other.
Magdela One thing you'll learn about me: I say what I think. You'll find out that Magdela is a very feisty lady.
Jeremy Feisty?
Magdela Feisty. That's what I am. A very feisty lady. Get that straight from the start.
Jeremy I'll just write it down. Can you spell feisty?
Magdela Who doesn't appreciate being made fun of. I created this business. It's Stock Exchange listed and makes a lot of money. So I know what I'm talking about. And when I go to the trouble of writing you a brief, I don't expect you still to write crap.
Jeremy I did try and follow your brief.
Magdela Are you saying my brief was crap?

Jeremy Heaven forbid. It was somewhat monosyllabic however. "This article has to be good" with "good" underlined three times, is less than totally informative.

Magdela I wrote that because I wanted it to be good. I told you exactly what I wanted.

Jeremy Well, all you actually told me was that you wanted it to be good.

Magdela And I went to the trouble of underlining "good" three times. I can't make it clearer than that, can I?

Jeremy Well, you could have said you wanted excellence.

Magdela I doubt if you can even spell excellence.

Jeremy No, I assure you ——

Magdela Now, look at this part.

Jeremy Yes, I'm talking about comedy here. The structure of jokes.

Magdela And you've written a sample joke.

Jeremy Yes, I quite liked that. If Mexican waves cheer up crowds, why don't they use them at funerals?

Magdela Are you really as stupid as you sound? This magazine goes to children. You don't talk about funerals to children. Their parents would be horrified. They want their children told that this is a lovely, fluffy world full of nice people who never die.

Jeremy Can't mention funerals?

Magdela Of course not. (*She scribbles out the joke*) What we write is: If Mexican waves cheer up crowds, why don't we use them on more solemn occasions?

Jeremy More solemn occasions?

Magdela More solemn occasions. Even you can see that's better, surely. Brainless halfwit though you obviously are.

Jeremy Oh, yes. Yes indeed. And of course where I refer to that film, *Four Weddings and a Funeral*, we'd better change that, hadn't we? *Four Weddings and a More Solemn Occasion*.

Magdela Right, that's it. I've got people to see who matter. I don't need to waste my time with fools. I'll have a word with Carol, don't expect her to send me congenital idiots. I'd say it was nice to meet you, if it was. (*She starts to leave*)

Jeremy No, look, I'm ... I didn't mean to be rude. I think I have a better

Scene 7

grasp now of what's required. I'm really grateful for your explanation. Thank you for making things so clear for me.

Magdela (*letting him lead her back*) I don't have to put up with infantile jokes from writers. Writers are two a penny. None of this stuff is the slightest use to me. There are a dozen young writers out there who will be grateful for the chance. Do you want the work or not?

Jeremy Yes. Yes, I see it as a challenge.

Magdela (*getting up to go*) All right. I'll have a word with Carol. But unless I like what I see next time, you're out on your ear. Magdela is a very feisty lady. Anyone will tell you that. I want it all re-written and on my desk by nine tomorrow morning. (*She moves towards the door then turns*) Did Carol tell me you once had a novel published?

Jeremy Yes.

Magdela Was that crap too?

Jeremy Well, some people thought it was rather good.

Magdela What was it called?

Jeremy *Trekking to Paradise.*

Magdela That tells me all I need to know about it. Young people in sleeping bags, none of them with any money and they think they're happy. Am I right?

Jeremy I'm afraid there was a little of that. But no funerals.

Magdela Just try to get it right next time. There won't be another chance.

Magdela exits. Miriam enters

Miriam She told you where to get off, didn't she? She's feisty, like she said.

Jeremy Only if feisty is a synonym for bullying. Were you listening at the door?

Miriam Why not? Wasn't secret, was it? Want to know what my sister's lover's up to.

Jeremy You know perfectly well I'm sleeping in the spare room.

Miriam Yes, quite a lot of them do that. Then they creep through. There's a floorboard that squeaks.

Jeremy Miriam, we haven't …

Miriam No, you were probably going to the bathroom. Are you staying long?

Jeremy I don't know. It doesn't look like it at the moment. Would you prefer I didn't?

Miriam Well, I don't know, really. Only Dad would hate it. He keeps bringing along Jewish men for her to inspect, and me too you know. He just wants to see one of us properly married to a nice Jewish boy, he doesn't care which one it is. It might be me first, not her. There must be something I can do better than her.

Jeremy You shouldn't put yourself down. I'll come and dance at your wedding.

Miriam Only if you're invited. I keep putting her lovers on the guest list, then taking them off when she drops them.

Jeremy You're writing a guest list? But you haven't decided who you're going to marry yet.

Miriam No, but when I do I'll have the guest list ready. It'll be one less thing to worry about.

Jeremy Am I on it now?

Miriam Well, yes, but only in pencil. I need to be able to rub you out without making a mess of the paper.

Jeremy Is it going to be a splendid wedding?

Miriam My dad's been putting money into a pot for our weddings ever since Ruth was born, so there's thousands of pounds now, and maybe Ruth isn't going to want her share. I mean, if you stayed, well, I can't quite imagine you in the middle of a great big Jewish wedding. You mightn't even get married. You're a bit sort of modern and bohemian, aren't you? So there'd be twice as much for mine. Not that I'm saying — I probably shouldn't talk like that — she'd ... I'm sorry, I'm saying the wrong thing again, aren't I?

Jeremy Not at all. Anyway, I'm probably not staying unless I can write something Magdela likes. If Ruth wants to know where I am, I'm upstairs, slaving over a hot laptop.

Jeremy exits

Black-out

Scene 8

The same. Carol and Ruth are on stage

Carol Darling. Darling Ruth, I don't mean it's hopeless. I can do something with him. But he's got to work with me.
Ruth He's upstairs now, re-writing all that stuff for Magdela.
Carol Bless him, the darling. Only you see, it's not enough.
Ruth He thinks the problem was that she didn't like what he wrote.
Carol It's not just that.
Ruth What is it then?
Carol Oh, darling, Magdela — well, darling, Magdela is one of my bestest, bestest clients, honestly, and I'm so pleased to have her on board, and I love her dearly, and if I lost her I'd be heartbroken.
Ruth And a lot poorer.
Carol Look, her fee income's important to the company. But it's personal, darling. You know how I feel about my clients. I think of Magdela as a friend — not like you of course, darling, but a friend all the same. It's not the same for you. You're a lawyer. You don't have to love your clients. Just come in Mr so-and-so, no you haven't a case, next. For us, well, I feel a personal commitment.
Ruth So, what is it about Magdela?
Carol Oh, darling, I feel disloyal saying this, but the thing is she's just the teeniest, teeniest bit of a tyrannical bully. Her staff are all terrified of her. Honestly. She's got this assistant, this mousy middle-aged woman who knows she'll never get another job, and this woman comes into meetings with her, and she always looks frightened, and sometimes Magdela will tear into her, just like that, make her look really, really small in front of everyone, and this woman, you can see her shaking. It's so funny to watch. (*She laughs quietly*)
Ruth It's not acceptable behaviour.
Carol (*shaking off the laughter*) No, of course, darling, it's absolutely unforgivable. Disgraceful. Of course it is.
Ruth Anyway, how does it affect Jeremy?
Carol Well, this is the thing, darling. Magdela feels he didn't treat her with respect. The more she thought about it afterwards, the more she thought he was laughing at her. And she wants a written apology.

Ruth What on earth for?

Carol Darling, put yourself in her shoes. She built this very profitable business, she's mistress of all she surveys. She's earned the right to be treated with respect. She doesn't like being laughed at.

Ruth Has this happened before?

Carol One of my designers. She didn't like the way he spoke to her. Thought he was having a private joke at her expense.

Ruth What did you do?

Carol I told him, if I didn't have his written apology to Magdela in my hands by five o'clock he could pick up his cards on his way home. Oh, Ruth, don't look at me like that. What else could I have done?

Ruth All right, I'll see what Jeremy wants to do.

Carol Darling, do try and get him to do what I want. You see, well, Magdela only saw him because I recommended him, and she might hold it against me if ... She's an important client. And of course, I only asked her to see him because you asked me to, and you're my bestest friend and I love you dearly.

Ruth I'll talk to him.

Carol I can't tell you how grateful I am. He's — he's terribly charming, isn't he, Jeremy?

Ruth Charming? Yes, in a rustic sort of way.

Carol I can see how attractive he must have been when you first met him. When he was young and successful, and he had the world at his feet before he went to seed in the countryside. He used to be the next big thing, didn't he? But darling, you do know, don't you, that that charming, talented, successful young man — You do know he's gone, forever? Darling, you once told me I was going to make a fool of myself over a man and I've never stopped being grateful, not for a moment.

Ruth That was rather different. When does he get out of prison, by the way?

Carol Not for years. Judges are really vindictive about fraud these days. But look, darling, Jeremy — I love him to bits, of course — but he's a terminal failure. There's nothing as catching as failure. You don't want to be near it. He'll never make any money. He doesn't even want to, except to please you. To make money, you've got to really, really want to. I'm only saying this because I care about you.

Scene 9   31

Ruth He's just an old friend now, and I'd like to help him if I can. Nothing more.

Black-out

SCENE 9

The same

Jeremy is sitting at the table reading and making corrections to a huge pile of papers in front of him

Ruth enters

Ruth Good. You're down at last. She's due any minute.
Jeremy Who?
Ruth Carol. To talk about the stuff you're going to give Magdela. And show her the draft of the letter you've done, apologizing to Magdela. We talked about that.
Jeremy Carol. Oh God. Oh God, I'd forgotten completely. Christ.
Ruth What's the matter? It's all fine. You've been working solidly, you've got reams of material written.
Jeremy Yes. Yes, of course. Of course.
Ruth Is there a problem?

The doorbell rings

   I'll go.

Ruth exits

Jeremy What am I going to do? (*He stares at his papers again in horror, then picks them up and tries to leave with them, but he is too late*)

Ruth and Carol enter

Carol Darling, Jeremy, Ruth gave me the wonderful news. Can I see? (*She takes the papers*)

Jeremy Wait. I mean ...

Carol goes through the papers. A look of puzzlement comes over her face. Jeremy stands in agitation behind her. Hold the moment for as long as the suspense will last

Ruth Is anything wrong?
Carol Jeremy, darling. Darling, Ruth. Jeremy, what are you going to do with this?
Jeremy Look, it's only work in progress. I was, look —I was going to change the names.
Ruth What on earth's going on?

She takes the papers from Carol

Carol You were in on this, Ruth, weren't you? I've never felt such a betrayal of trust. Never.
Ruth (*reading*) "Carol nailed a smile to the plastic of her face and slithered into the room, scattering 'darlings' like confetti." (*Looking up*) Jeremy, this isn't an article for Magdela's magazine, is it?
Jeremy No. No, I'm afraid it isn't.
Ruth You haven't done a stroke of work on that, have you?
Jeremy Not what you might call work, no. I haven't written a word for it.
Ruth This is the next novel, isn't it?
Jeremy Look, I ought to explain, Carol. Look, that character isn't you. Not entirely, anyway. And Magdela isn't Magdela.
Carol There's a Magdela? God! (*She grabs the manuscript back from Ruth and starts going through it*)
Jeremy She's not Magdela, she just has some of Magdela's characteristics.
Carol (*reading*) "Magdela gave him the sort of look you'd see on a viper which had just spotted a tasty snack whose legs were too short to run away."
Jeremy Look, she's only called Magdela here because — I mean, in the end she'll probably be called Melissa or something.

Scene 9

Carol How could you?
Ruth This is ten times as much as you've written in the last ten years. What was missing all that time?
Jeremy You were missing, Ruth.
Ruth Oh, come on.
Jeremy I don't mean you as a lover. I mean you as a character. I mean, you were missing, and so was Carol and Miriam. So were Gary and Hugh, so was Magdela. I couldn't work without them. I was sitting in my little room in Solva and looking at the raging sea and the huge, glowering cliffs, and walking round the wonderful countryside, and thinking that was where a writer got his inspiration from. And that was all rubbish. I needed to be here in London, looking at greed and hypocrisy made flesh.
Carol Thank you very much.
Jeremy I worked in my little room, and their voices got fainter, until I could hardly hear them any more. Without them I have nothing to write.
Carol Jeremy, I know the best libel lawyers in London. If a single word of this appears anywhere, I promise you faithfully ——
Ruth It's easy to make it libel-proof.

The doorbell rings

(*Shouting*) Miriam, get that, can you? It'll be Gary.
Jeremy Gary? What does he want?
Ruth I told you, he's here for an answer. He's a bit early, but the way this discussion is going, I can't see that it matters.

Gary enters

Gary, you've met Carol?
Gary Have I met Carol! There isn't a Labour politician in London who doesn't know the wonderful Carol, not a politician who matters anyway. Where do you think we get our slogans from? "Excellence From Innovation" — that was one of Carol's master strokes.
Carol (*with an effort*) Darling, Gary! My very favourite rising politician.

They kiss extravagantly on both cheeks

    Darling, Ruth, Gary is really so brilliant, I could eat him. He's tipped as the next Prime Minister but three, did you know that?
Gary So, have you thought about that contract?
Jeremy Gary, I've thought about practically nothing else since we last talked.
Ruth (*pointing to the papers*) You mean Gary's in here? You haven't included the offer he made you — thirty thousand pounds a year to keep *shtum* about a school scandal?
Jeremy Chapters two, four and seven. It's a key point in the plot.
Ruth Then you're certainly not signing his contract, are you? You're writing about it instead.
Gary Will someone bring me up to speed on this?
Ruth Jeremy's writing a novel. You seem to have provided some useful dramatic material. He'll change the names, of course. Though most reviewers will see through that.
Gary I see. (*To Carol*) Can he get it published, do you think?
Carol Yes. He's still young and good-looking enough to be marketable. I tried his name out on a publisher friend of mine. He called him "The Mystery Man". They've been waiting years for his second novel, apparently. If it's any good, they'll eat it up.
Jeremy Not to mention serialization in the Sunday papers.
Carol Now, darling, you're bit out of your league there.
Ruth You've been talking to my agent friend, haven't you, Jeremy?
Jeremy Well, it's just —
Ruth You haven't put some Americans in for her, have you?
Jeremy No, but she said the Gary character would do instead. Politicians are almost as good as Americans, apparently. Not quite, but nearly. Politicians do what Americans tell them to do.
Gary Right. I've heard enough. You listen to me.

Miriam enters in a rush

Miriam Oh, that was so hard, you've no idea. I mean, just try to get a lively two-year-old to sleep when there are all these exciting people here. And Gary, of course he heard Gary's voice.

Scene 9

Gary Thank you, Miriam, helpful as always. Listen to me, Jezza. You need to forget all about this, right now. You're in deeper than you know. You may think we can't touch you. But we can hurt you in ways you'll never trace. All you'll know is that suddenly editors don't return your calls, publishers don't get round to reading your manuscripts, no one wants to know you.

Carol I'd listen to Gary if I were you, Jeremy. Darling, Ruth, save him from himself, for heaven's sake.

Miriam Have I interrupted something?

Jeremy Gary and Carol seem to think I ought not to get my new novel published, that's all.

Miriam Oh, Jeremy, think about it sensibly. I mean Gary's an awfully important man and he's in the government and all that, and Carol's so clever and so pretty and everyone thinks the world of her, and well you've just got to listen to them. I mean, it stands to reason.

Gary Stop wittering, Miriam, you sound like a demented barn owl.

Ruth Don't speak to Miriam like that.

Gary You always do.

Ruth That's different, she's my sister.

Gary Look, Ruth, you're an intelligent woman, or at least you used to be in the days when you and I fucked ourselves to sleep every night — Sorry, Jeremy, didn't you know about that? Miriam never blurted it out before? Shouldn't have opened my big mouth, naughty Gary. Still, it's out now.

Ruth You fucked yourself to sleep, Gary. I just had a strange sensation that a wooden wardrobe had fallen on top of me, and some fool left the key in the lock. That was on good nights. Bad nights, I could spend hours looking for the key.

Gary Ruth, Ruth, I don't want us to quarrel. Just tell your friend to be a sensible lad, and not only will no harm come to him, we'll actually put a bit of money into his miserable life. Thirty years old and he lives in a bloody rented flat, for God's sake.

Ruth Jeremy, listen to me. Gary wants you to behave like a sensible lad, take the money, destroy the novel, keep your schoolboy secrets to yourself. Gary's got powerful friends. He's also offering thirty thousand pounds a year for not a lot of work.

Jeremy Do you think I ought to do it then?

Ruth Carol also wants you to behave like a sensible lad. She can put a substantial contract your way so long as you destroy the novel, make a grovelling apology to Magdela, and in future behave towards Magdela with the respect due to someone who's awfully rich. Carol's offering a substantial contract too.
Carol Twenty thousand pounds a year.
Ruth Thirty thousand pounds, wasn't it?
Carol Yes, of course.
Ruth There's sixty thousand pounds even without your friend Hugh. So what do you want to do?
Jeremy What I want is to stay here forever with you and Ben. So I've got to be sensible, haven't I? You don't want a man living with you who's not sensible.
Gary That's it, Jeremy. If you want Ruth, you learn to behave like a sensible lad. She knows the world. If she's with you, she'll be damned by association.
Carol Darling Jeremy, you and Ruth are so good together, I can tell how much in love you are. I mean it would be criminal to destroy that. Ruth, I said before, didn't I, how wonderful it would be if you could get him to stay with you.
Jeremy Ruth, what am I going to do?
Ruth You're going to make a decision, Jeremy. I can't make it for you. I think you've already made it.
Miriam I mean, think about it, Jeremy, I know you think the world of her, and all that, and that's wonderful, of course it is, but I mean, love isn't everything, is it, and I mean, think of me. I'm the piggy in the middle here, and what would I tell Daddy? I mean, I'd have had enough trouble with Gary, and he's got a high-powered job and all that.
Ruth Miriam, when I want your advice I'll ask for it. Jeremy?
Jeremy All right. Carol, Gary, look, I'm really grateful to you, both of you. Really I am. You're both being very generous. And at any other time I'd be really grateful, only just now, you see, I've got this novel to finish, and that's going to keep me very busy for quite a time.
Gary You'll live to regret that decision.

Gary exits

Scene 9

Carol Ruth, if our friendship means anything at all to you, you'll change his mind for him.

Carol kisses Ruth, kisses Miriam, and after a moment's hesitation kisses Jeremy, then exits

Jeremy I'm not a *mensch*, you see. I'll get my rucksack and head back to Solva.
Ruth A *mensch* doesn't let events dictate to him. He takes a decision. That's what you've just done.
Jeremy Can a novelist be a *mensch*?
Ruth So long as he's serious, yes.
Miriam You mean he's staying?
Ruth You know what writers are like, Miriam. They find a place where they can work, and then that's where they have to be. So I'm afraid we're stuck with him.
Miriam Well, looking on the bright side, you two won't want a wedding so I can have one twice as big. Not being greedy but I mean that's just realistic, isn't it? You know what, I'm going to ink in Jeremy's name on my wedding invitation list now, because I don't think I'm going to have to rub it out. I mean I hate rubbing them out. I shouldn't have said that, should I?

Black-out

THE END

FURNITURE AND PROPERTY LIST

Scene 1

On stage: Coffee table. *On it*: coasters
Two chairs with cushions

Off stage: Rucksack containing noteboook, papers, pen and small pocket diary (**Jeremy**)
Two cups of tea (**Ruth**)

Scene 2

Set: Bottle of wine and two glasses on the table

Scene 3

Off stage: Tray. *On it*: three mugs of coffee (**Miriam**)

Scene 4

Off stage: Bottle of Armagnac and two glasses (**Jeremy**)

Scene 5

Off stage: Mug of coffee (**Ruth**)

Scene 6

Off stage: Bundle of papers (**Gary**)

Personal: **Carol**: bag containing papers

Scene 7

On stage: Sheets of paper (**Magdela**)

Furniture and Property List

SCENE 8

No props required

SCENE 9

Set: Pile of papers on table

LIGHTING PLOT

Scene 1

To open: Interior lighting

Cue 1	**Jeremy**: "I always hated it when she did that." *Black-out*	(Page 5)

Scene 2

To open: Interior lighting

Cue 2	**Ruth** takes the wine and glasses and exits *Black-out*	(Page 8)

Scene 3

To open: Interior lighting

Cue 3	**Ruth**: "... I don't want you getting comfortable here." *Black-out*	(Page 10)

Scene 4

To open: Interior lighting

Cue 4	**Ruth** appears in her dressing gown, looking thunderous *Black-out*	(Page 14)

Scene 5

To open: Interior lighting

Cue 5	**Ruth** exits *Black-out*	(Page 15)

Lighting Plot

SCENE 6

To open: Interior lighting

Cue 6	**Gary** exits. **Ruth** and **Jeremy** look at each other *Black-out*	(Page 25)

SCENE 7

To open: Interior lighting

Cue 7	**Jeremy** exits *Black-out*	(Page 28)

SCENE 8

To open: Interior lighting

Cue 8	**Ruth**: "... help him if I can. Nothing more." *Black-out*	(Page 31)

SCENE 9

To open: Interior lighting

Cue 9	**Miriam**: "I shouldn't have said that, should I?" *Black-out*	(Page 37)

EFFECTS PLOT

Cue 1	**Carol** exits *Door slams*	(Page 20)
Cue 2	**Jeremy** stands, uncertain, leafing through the papers *Doorbell rings*	(Page 20)
Cue 3	**Ruth**: "Is there a problem?" *Doorbell rings*	(Page 31)
Cue 4	**Ruth**: "It's easy to make it libel-proof." *Doorbell rings*	(Page 33)

www.ingramcontent.com/pod-product-compliance
Lightning Source LLC
Chambersburg PA
CBHW070637050426
42450CB00011B/3235